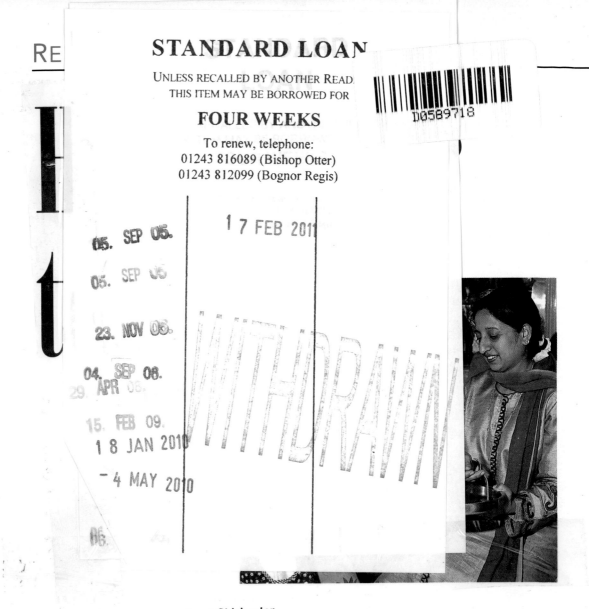

Carrie Mercier

Oxfor

About the series

We live in a world where there are people of many different religions. In many of our towns and cities Buddhists, Christians and Jews live alongside Muslims, Hindus and Sikhs. If you travel abroad, you will soon experience whole countries that have been shaped by religion.

We all have different ways of looking at things. It could be said that we all see the world through our own "spectacles". These spectacles are made up of our beliefs, opinions, attitudes and values. What is important to you might not be important to me.

Religious people see the world through their spectacles, which affects the way they see and live in the world. We can't understand someone else's worldview unless we look through their spectacles. The *Religion for Today* series helps you to do this by giving you the skills and knowledge to understand people with beliefs different from your own.

In learning about another religion you will also be given the chance to think about your own life. So you will not only learn about the religions you study, you will also learn from the religions.

Chris Wright, Series Editor

About this book

This book offers an introduction to the beliefs and practices of Hindus in the world today. It will help you explore responses to some of the deeper questions in life — ones that Hindus find answered in the stories and traditions of their faith. For example, how did the universe begin, why do people suffer, what happens after death, how should we live our lives? The book will also help you to approach the beliefs and practices of people from different religions with understanding, respect and a readiness to learn from others.

Many of the beliefs and practices of Hindus may at first appear unfamiliar. This book will help you to see connections between your own experiences and those of the believers. In this way you will see how religions express and respond to universal human needs and experiences.

Carrie Mercier

Practical hints

Learning the correct vocabulary is important in finding out about a religion. Many of the words used in this book are in the Sanskrit language, the ancient language of the Hindu scriptures. You will find a list of a number of these words, and their meaning, in the Glossary on page 62. You may come across different spellings in other books — for example the goddess Lakshmi may appear as Laksmi, Aum as Om, Shiva as Siva. Try to use only one form of spelling in your writing.

Contents

one

S*tarting out*

In this unit you will think about where to begin with the study of a religion. You will find out where Hinduism began.

1 *Imagine you had to do a project on a) your school, b) your town or village, c) your family, d) your local football team, where would you begin? Would you start with the history of the village, the foundation of the school, your family tree, the first members of the team or would you begin with the way things are now? Discuss each of your answers with a partner.*

" In India there are many different languages and cultural traditions. Religious practice varies from place to place too. The majority of people in India today are Hindu. "
[*Anita, 15*]

Most religions, like most communities and families, have roots or foundations that go back a long way. Hinduism has roots that go back nearly six thousand years. The word Hinduism comes from the name of the River Indus. This river is in the north-west of the Indian sub-continent. Some people say that Hinduism has its earliest roots here.

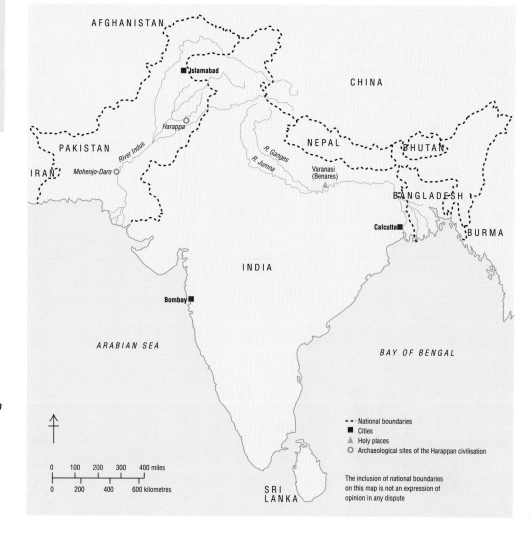

Look at the map. Make a mental note of the shape of the Indian sub-continent. Look at where the River Indus is. Now cover the map and draw a sketch of the Indian sub-continent from memory. Put in the River Indus. Check your map and label it. Write a sentence under it to explain where Hinduism has its roots.

The religion we call Hinduism developed over thousands of years. Hinduism cannot be defined in a single set of beliefs and there is great variety in the way Hindus practise their religion. Hindus would say that although they appear to be doing different things they are all on the same path. However, they are travelling in different ways and they are at different stages along the road.

Although Hinduism has its origins in India, it is now a world faith. Its influence has spread. Today there are Hindu communities living in many parts of the world and Hinduism is one of the principal world religions in the United Kingdom.

❝ I worship at the temple with my mother. Sometimes my father joins us. My grandmother worships at home at the shrine. My brother goes to classes on yoga and meditation. He says he prefers this to worshipping in the temple.
[*Sita, 12*]

We call our religion Sanatan Dharma. Sanatan means eternal. Dharma means what is right. Hinduism is about trying to do what is right. ❞
[*Sangit, 13*]

left: A Hindu making offerings at a shrine in India.

right: A Hindu priest making offerings at a shrine in the UK.

2 *Look at the photos. Write down the differences and similarities you can see between these two acts of worship. Suggest reasons for the differences. Discuss your answers in class.*

3 *Design a title page to introduce your work on Hinduism. Use the photos and the quotations to help you.*

4 *Look at the photos and read the quotations again. Write six sentences to explain what you have learnt about Hinduism in this unit. Read through what you have written to a friend or partner. Add to your work if you think you have missed some important information.*

two

Understanding the truth

Most people put their trust in the world of material things. They look for security in a house. They make money and fill their lives with possessions. Their idea of reality is limited to the material world and they expect it to make them happy.

1
(a) *Advertisers use ideas of security, reliability and happiness to sell their goods. Collect pictures from magazines to illustrate this trust in the material world and tendency to look for happiness in possessions. Compare your pictures and advertisements with those of a friend or partner. Discuss the messages given in the pictures.*

(b) *Money may not last, cars rust, houses and possessions can be destroyed or taken away. Show this in a collage/poster using your pictures. Write a few sentences under your artwork to explain how your picture gets this message across.*

> ❝ What is real, what is lasting, what will be there when everything else has disappeared or has been destroyed? If there is something, then that is what we should trust in. ❞
> [*Indi, 18*]

Hindus believe it is a mistake to treat the material world as if it can bring security or lasting happiness. They believe that real happiness comes from knowing Brahman. Brahman is the Supreme Spirit. Brahman is real — but not in the same way as the objects we know through our senses. Hindus say we cannot see Brahman with our ordinary eyes, yet Brahman is present everywhere and in everything.

Do advertisers tell us what will make us happy?

❝ Some Hindus call Brahman Ultimate Reality. They say Brahman is more real than the physical world because Brahman is eternal and unchanging.
[*Asha, 16*]

Brahman is the Supreme Spirit of the Universe. Brahman is in everything. Brahman is present in all living things. ❞
[*Shiv, 14*]

2 *Write the word Brahman in the centre of a page. Then write the quotations above putting them into speech bubbles. Leave space between them. Invent questions to which these quotes could be answers and write them in the spaces. Add further questions and answers to show your understanding of the word "Brahman".*

3 *Write a short play of a debate between someone who says that the material world is all that matters and someone who believes that what matters is another reality, they may call it "Spirit", "God", "Ultimate Reality" or "Brahman" – it is up to you.*

We rely on the sun to rise again every morning but one day even the sun and moon will pass away.

THREE

Finding the soul within

In this unit you will consider the questions "What is the real me?" and "Do I have a soul or spirit?" You will also learn about what Hindus have to say on these issues.

1 (a) *What is the "real you" like? Ask a friend to describe you as they see and know you. Write your own description of what you are like. Compare the two descriptions. Discuss the differences with your partner. What does this tell you?*

(b) *Is the "you" that people see, the "outside you", the real you? Is there a "you" inside that is different? Take a whole page, and using words and pictures illustrate the outside you and the inside you. Explain your drawing in one or two sentences.*

It is hard to say exactly what is the real self. Some people would say that the body is an important part of what makes you "you". Yet the body changes. You do not have the same body you had as a baby. So where do we look when we want to get to the "real" in you? Is it your feelings, your mind, your memories, your personality? Questions such as these have challenged thinkers in every age and in every culture.

2 *Describe the changes you have experienced in your life since the age of five. Indicate the ways in which you have changed physically and ways in which you have developed in terms of feelings, character, interests and outlook. Say what remains unchanged.*

Hindus believe that every person, in fact every living creature, has a soul. This soul is the real you.

❝ It is not those things that make us individual that are real – our bodies, our feelings and emotions all change in time. Our character is the result of our experiences and so this is not permanent either. Only the spirit or soul is permanent. ❞
[*Moti, 17*]

What gives us our sense of identity – of who we are?

Hindus believe that the soul is eternal and unchanging. Not only will it continue to exist after physical death, but it existed before we were born. Hindus call this soul atman. Atman is spirit as Brahman is spirit.

> " You see people trying to establish their personal identity through the way they dress, through their job or career or even their relationships. But this identity is temporary. It is not the real self. The true self is atman. "
> [Gupta, 16]

3 *What are the different ways in which people try to find an identity? In a cartoon strip or story use words and pictures to illustrate the idea of "The search for the true self."*

Some Hindus say that atman and Brahman are one and the same. In other words the Supreme Spirit is present within us. Others say that atman is Spirit like Brahman but it is not identical with Brahman because Brahman is greater than atman.

> " If we really believed that God is within us, we would not look for happiness in the material world, we would look within ourselves to find eternal peace and happiness. "
> [Roma, 16]

4 *Working in a small group, write a short radio discussion on the nature of the soul – make one of the voices a Hindu. Try to bring in some of the ideas expressed in this unit. Record your radio programme or read it out to the rest of the class.*

This Hindu holy man only possesses what he can carry with him on his travels.

FOUR

Meditating

In this unit you will consider the times when you want to just be left alone to be still or reflect on things. You will learn about the Hindu practice of meditation and how yoga is used to help in meditation.

Being still and quiet is not easy in today's busy world. Television programmes rush from one item to the next. Information technology and computer programs get faster and faster. People often travel thousands of miles in a day and meals have become "fast food". There is little time to stop in order to be quiet and to reflect.

 Do you like to just be still sometimes? Perhaps you like to lie on your back and watch the clouds. Or you may not like being quiet at all. Perhaps you prefer to be on the move all the time. Write a poem or short essay called "Being Still" which explores your thoughts and feelings on this.

In Hinduism being still is an important part of religious life. Many Hindus meditate each day. Meditation can mean just being still and quiet to find the silence within. It may involve reciting a mantra, which is a prayer or sacred chant.

For some Hindus a yantra or special pattern is used to focus and still the busy mind.

> *Aum, this eternal word is all; what was, what is and what shall be, and what beyond is eternity. All is Aum.*
> [*from The Upanishads*]

Many Hindus meditate each day.

Some Hindus use a yantra to focus and still the mind.

>
>
> " People seem to be afraid to stop and be still. They must always be busy doing something. Our religion teaches us to find the truth that lies in silence and being still.
> [Ela, 41]
>
> I spend two hours a day in meditation. The best time is early in the morning when it is quiet. "
> [Kavita, 17]

The sacred sound and symbol aum.

Some Hindus use yoga. "Yoga" means "yoke" or "discipline". It is intended to help control the body and the mind so that a person can become free from selfishness, greed, impatience and anxiety. Yoga begins with restraint in everyday thoughts and actions.

> " People think yoga means learning peculiar positions for keeping fit. But true yoga begins with curbing greed, selfishness and wrongdoing. It doesn't matter how clever you are at the lotus position. If you lie and cheat or you are full of hatred or envy you cannot be truly still or at peace.
> [Tilak, 15]
>
> When you begin to meditate you can concentrate on simple exercises like learning to sit properly and learning to control your breathing. Then you can begin to be more in control of your mind, thoughts and feelings. "
> [Nirmal, 13]

 Try a class exercise in the first steps of meditation. Sit in a comfortable position and become calm and still. Imagine your head is held up by a string so that the back is straight but not rigid. Look down or close your eyes. Concentrate on the point where the air enters the nose. Breathe gently and steadily. Remain silent for one minute keeping your mind on the air entering and leaving the body. Let other thoughts pass by unattended. After one minute stop and discuss with the person next to you what the exercise was like. Try the exercise again, but for five minutes. Write a detailed account of the experience. Say what you think you learnt from it.

FIVE

Worshipping

In this unit you will reflect on the meaning of the word worship. You will also find out about some of the ways in which Hindus worship.

 What do you understand by the word worship? What sort of activities might worship include? Draw a spider diagram to represent your ideas and the connections between them.

Hindus worship in different ways. Sometimes worship will involve making offerings at a shrine. Sometimes it involves singing hymns and saying prayers. It may include playing music or chanting words from the scriptures. Worship can be a matter of private, individual devotion. It can also be a group activity such as in a gathering for a festival or place of pilgrimage.

Hindus call worship "puja". For most Hindus, daily worship takes place at a shrine. The shrine usually contains an image (murti) of a deity. This may take the form of a statue or a picture.

> ❝ When we perform puja we offer gifts of food, light, incense and prayer at the shrine in our home. The shrine contains an image of Lord Krishna. For me Krishna represents God as a friend.
> [Arjun, 11]
>
> The image in our shrine is Shiva. Shiva represents God for me. He is the Lord of all. I pray to him and ask him for forgiveness for things I've done wrong and for help and protection. ❞
> [Dipa, 12]

The images used in worship are symbols representing God or different aspects of God's power and presence. Before Hindus approach the shrine they remove their shoes. At the shrine they put their hands together and bow. In this way they show respect and reverence. Thirteen-year-old Leela said: "God is present everywhere but sometimes we need a reminder of God's presence and a focus for prayer. The image of the deity helps us to put God first in our thoughts."

 The images Hindus use in worship represent aspects of God such as love, wisdom, truth and the power to overcome evil. Describe or illustrate two images or pictures that are important in your life or meaningful for you. Say why they are important and what they represent.

In daily worship, flowers and incense are offered at the shrine. Often a bell is rung. Yellow turmeric, red kum kum powder and sandalwood paste are used to anoint the images. Gifts of fruit and sweets are offered. The worshipper may touch the feet of the image as a sign of respect and devotion.

> 66 Our scriptures tell us that we may offer a leaf or a flower. If we offer it with love it is acceptable to God. God sees what is in our hearts and knows whether our worship is sincere or empty.
> [Kiran, 12]
>
> We do not worship just with words. We offer our thoughts and prayers of course, but also our feelings and our senses. In fact what we are offering is ourselves. This is what the offerings of puja are saying. 99
> [Manoj, 14]

3 ▶ *The senses are important in Hindu worship. Make a 3D collage on the theme of worship – using things that smell sweet, different colours and textures, and cut-out pictures and patterns. Write a label to go with your artwork to explain its meaning.*

4 ▶ *Write a paragraph describing what you see happening in the photo. Include as much detail as you can. Choose one of the quotations above to include in your description of Hindu puja. Explain what the quotation tells you about Hindu worship.*

Puja usually involves making offerings at a shrine.

SIX

Honouring God as Mother

People often use stories to talk about God. You may know stories in which God is described as a father or a king for example.

 What words are used to describe God? Make a page of thought bubbles and pictures to show the different ways that people think about and talk about God.

Stories can be symbolic and explore meanings and ideas that are hard to explain in other ways. In Hinduism there are many stories which deal with the battle between the forces of good and evil. In this story God's power is represented as a female force called "Durga". Durga's face is mild and beautiful but when it comes to protecting the world and all living creatures she is fierce and frightening:

The goddess appears in different form. Here she has three faces representing different aspects of her nature.

An evil demon was ravaging the world destroying all that was good and leaving chaos behind. The powers of heaven and earth called upon Durga to save the world from destruction. Mounted on a tiger, with a different weapon in each of her ten hands, Durga came to the rescue. The demon changed its form to try to escape the powers of Durga. First it was a buffalo, then a raging elephant, then a giant with a thousand arms. However, Durga was invincible. She killed the demon with a lance through his heart. Peace and harmony were restored to the earth and everyone gave thanks to Durga for saving them.

2 *The powers of evil and destruction do seem to change form. In each age there is a new threat to the world. What are the destructive forces at work in the world today? Write a modern version of the story of Durga in which she overcomes some of these.*

Every year Hindus celebrate Durga Puja. An image of Durga is made of clay. She is dressed for the occasion and becomes the focus of worship. At the end of the festival the image is carried in a procession to a lake or river where it is immersed to return to the clay of the riverbed. The image has served its purpose. God is greater than the image itself.

> " At Durga Puja we take offerings to the temple and put them before the image of Durga. Durga holds up her hand as if to say: Do not fear. She has the power to protect us. "
> [*Bharat, 11*]

3 *Is it just as helpful to talk of God as Mother as it is to talk of God as Father? Arrange a class debate on this issue and write up the main arguments, concluding with your own.*

4 *What are the qualities of a good mother? Design a poster of the ideal mother. She can have many hands – she probably needs them. Write a paragraph explaining your picture.*

The Mother Goddess appears in different forms. As Parvati she is the beautiful and devoted wife of Lord Shiva. As Lakshmi she is the goddess of good fortune. She also appears as Saraswati the goddess of learning. In her most terrifying form she is Kali who is seen destroying the powers of evil.

5 *What skills and powers do we need in order to overcome evil in the world today? How would you represent these skills in a picture of a goddess for the future? Design such a goddess and explain it in a short talk or notes to accompany your picture.*

At Durga Puja the image is carried in a procession to a lake or river.

earing God

In this unit you will think about how the powers of destruction and creativity are often linked. You will also learn how this idea is expressed through the Hindu god Shiva.

Sometimes something has to be destroyed before there can be a new beginning. A block of flats is demolished in order to make room for new housing, or a fire destroys a forest but nature returns and flowers flourish where there was only blackened earth. Sometimes, even when the destruction has been unplanned and unwanted something new and creative springs from the wreckage. This connection between the powers of destruction and re-creation is captured in the Hindu god Shiva.

 Think of examples of destruction being followed by new life and new growth, or think of an occasion when something good has come out of something bad in your experience. Write a poem or story on this idea.

Hindus find images of God helpful because they remind them of the different aspects of God's power. Lord Shiva is often portrayed as a holy man smeared in ashes, deep in meditation, seated in a yoga position in the forests of the Himalayas. It is through long years of meditation that

he generates his mighty powers. He has a third eye in the centre of his forehead. It is said that, once, his wife Parvati crept up behind him in fun and put her beautiful hands over his eyes. By mistake she covered this third eye and the world was thrown into darkness. The earth trembled in fear awaiting the return of Shiva's power.

Often Shiva is represented by a smooth rounded stone. This is called a lingam. It stands for Shiva's power to regenerate the world and fill it with life.

Hindus making offerings to Lord Shiva.

" In our temple a white bull guards the shrine of Shiva. When we worship we pour milk over the Shiva lingam. We pray that he will accept our offering and look kindly upon us. Shiva has the power to destroy all things and to re-create them again. "
[*Prahlad, 15*]

2 *Some of the great life-giving forces in the world are also the most destructive. Write down four examples. Share your ideas in class and add to the examples you have chosen. Design a symbol that represents the power to both destroy and create.*

In one well-known image Shiva is dancing in a circle of flames, his hair flying out in all directions. He is trampling on the dwarf of ignorance. In his hand he beats a drum to keep the rhythm of the ever-turning universe.

"" We have a night dedicated to Shiva called Shivaratri. My mother and I fast all night. We take offerings to Lord Shiva's shrine at the temple. We sing hymns and the priest performs the puja. Afterwards we celebrate with a huge feast. ""
[*Manu, 11*]

3 *Lord Shiva is worshipped with great reverence and respect. Why do you think Hindus feel that he is such an important deity? Choose one image of Shiva and design a card inviting Hindus to the celebration of Shivaratri. Inside write a few words about Shivaratri as if the card were being sent by a Hindu to a good friend who is not Hindu.*

Shiva dancing: Identify the circle of flames, the dwarf of ignorance and the small drum with which Shiva keeps the rhythm of the universe.

EIGHT

Trusting in God as Friend

1 *What kind of friend would you like to be? What qualities would you like to develop in order to be a good friend to someone? Discuss your ideas in class. Write an article for a young person's magazine on what it means to be a good friend.*

There are many stories in Hinduism which encourage the worshipper to see God as a friend. This one is about Lord Vishnu who lived on earth as Krishna the cowherd in the forests of Vrindavan:

Lord Krishna shelters the people and calms their fears.

Long ago when Krishna was a youth a terrible storm threatened the land and the lives of the people of Vrindavan. Torrential rains fell for many days, the river became swollen and flooded its banks. Trees were being swept away and still the rains did not stop. The people turned to Krishna for help. Without any effort he lifted up a mountain with his little finger and sheltered the people until the rains stopped. All the people gave thanks to their friend for his help in their time of need. For a moment they wondered at his extraordinary powers but they never realised who he was. To them he was their friend and neighbour. Hindus today believe that Krishna was Vishnu in human form who came to earth to overcome evil and restore righteousness.

According to the Hindu scriptures Vishnu has come down to earth in many different forms. These incarnations or "descents" are called avatars. In each age Vishnu takes on a different form to come to earth to restore righteousness. Both Rama and Krishna are avatars of Vishnu. According to Hindu tradition there is one more avatar still to come, Kalki, riding on a white horse with a sword in his hand.

Radha and Krishna. What do Hindus learn from their story?

66 We worship Lord Vishnu and our temple is dedicated to Krishna. We have a shrine with an image of Krishna playing the flute. The stories tell us he used to play this when he was looking after the cows in Vrindavan.
[Sanjey, 10]

The stories of Krishna remind us that we must rely on God completely. No one else can give us the strength to face difficulty and overcome evil. We pray to Krishna as a friend and try to put our trust in him. 99
[Tara, 14]

In the stories of his life in Vrindavan, Krishna's closest friend is Radha. Radha adores Krishna. When he is away from her she feels lost and hurt and does not know what to do. In this way she learns to trust him and her love becomes stronger. Hindus say that they must learn to trust in God.

2 ▶ Sometimes being a friend is very hard. Sometimes it can hurt. With a partner discuss the times when being a friend is difficult. What can be learnt from these experiences? Design a symbol to represent friendship and trust.

3 ▶ Tell the story of Krishna and the rains in words and pictures. Say what the message of the story is for Hindus today.

oing to the temple

In this unit you will consider how certain places and buildings have an important place in the lives of people. You will learn about the place and importance of the temple for Hindus.

 (a) *People claim that the shopping centre has become the temple in people's lives. What do they mean? Can you think of other "temples"? Collect pictures from magazines to illustrate this idea. Make a class collage of modern temples.*

(b) *Where is the temple in your life? Which place or building houses that which is most important to you? Draw and label your temple or write a short description of the place.*

Many Hindus worship at a temple. The temple is called a "mandir". In India the temple is a home or house for a god or goddess. Going to the temple is up to the individual. No one has to go. Some people go to see the deity, to take offerings and to pray. People gather at the temple at festivals or on pilgrimage or at other times of celebration.

In India the mandir usually houses only one deity. In the United Kingdom the mandir may have several shrines dedicated to different deities such as Shiva, Vishnu and Durga. The images are usually brilliantly decorated and are the focal point of the prayer hall. Before the worshippers enter the prayer hall they take off their shoes for cleanliness and to show respect for the purity of the temple.

> ❝ I go to the temple to pray and to focus on God. God can easily get pushed to the edge of our lives. The temple is the place where God gets put back in the centre where he belongs.
> [Champa, 14]
>
> I go to the temple to worship God. I also go to meet my friends and to be with people from the same culture and background. ❞
> [Jyoti, 12]

Every mandir has a shrine where the image is housed. This has a roof or canopy over it. There will also be a prayer hall or space where people can sit or stand for worship. There are no chairs; worshippers sit on the floor. In the United Kingdom some temples have a community centre with a hall for weddings and other gatherings. There may be classrooms, kitchens and facilities for senior citizens, youth clubs and playgroups.

above: There is usually a priest (brahmin) at the mandir. This mandir is in India.

left: Many Hindus in the UK gather for worship at a mandir.

2 *What are the main differences between the temple in India and one in the United Kingdom? Look at the photos to help you. Suggest reasons for the differences. Write your answer under the heading "The Hindu temple – in India and in the United Kingdom."*

" Once a week we have a meal after our worship at our mandir. This is a time when we can all meet and talk. We all bring gifts of food and money which we place before the deities. This is used to provide the meal for everyone. "
[*Anita, 15*]

There is usually a priest at the temple. He looks after the images and performs puja at the shrine. In temples in the United Kingdom the priest leads the congregation and recites the prayers during worship. He is also able to perform the rituals required for a wedding ceremony or at a cremation.

3 *Prepare an information sheet for school parties visiting a Hindu mandir. Explain what you would find at a temple. Say how the temple is used and why it is important for Hindus. Illustrate your information sheet with diagrams, plans or pictures.*

ten

Receiving the light

In this unit you will think about symbolic gestures and actions and their meaning. You will also learn about the symbolism of the Hindu arti service.

Communication other than by using words is important. We communicate as much through our facial expressions, the movements of our hands and bodies as we do through our speech. In fact we are so used to communicating through body language that we even use it when we are on the telephone!

1 ► With a friend or partner discuss six examples of people using symbolic actions, hand signals and gestures to communicate (but not to insult!). Say why you think people communicate in this way in each case. Draw diagrams with explanations on six symbolic actions of this kind.

These women are performing arti at the shrine in their home. Looking at their body language, what can you tell about the meaning and importance of their actions?

Hindu rituals often involve symbolic actions that communicate the feelings or intentions of the worshipper. Arti is a welcoming ritual performed at the shrine. It may involve the offering of water, light, flowers and incense. In many temples in the United Kingdom arti has become a regular part of community worship.

When arti is performed at the mandir the priest prepares the deities for worship. They are washed and anointed with kum kum powder and sandalwood paste. Flowers, incense, food, water and other offerings are presented to the deities. Often the worshippers sit and sing hymns ("bhajans"), ring bells and play music. When the priest lights the arti lamp the congregation stands. The lamp has five flames. It is held up before the shrines and moved in a circle in front of each image. The priest then turns and faces the people and again moves the lamp in a circle before the congregation.

Receiving the light at the arti ceremony.

> ❝ We offer light at the shrine because we must offer everything we have and light is one of our most precious possessions. It is life and heat and the light of knowledge. ❞
> [*Prashant, 14*]

The lamp is taken round the congregation. Each person receives the light by drawing the palms of their hands across the top of the flame and then over the face and hair.

> ❝ I feel that when we receive the light we are receiving God's blessing and love. We accept the light and say thank you.
> [*Manjula, 14*]
>
> Going to the arti service is important for me. It helps me to remember that true enlightenment only comes from God. ❞
> [*Renu, 13*]

At the end of the service food is given to each worshipper. This is called prashad (blessed food). It is accepted as a gift from God and a reminder of the sweetness of God's love.

2 *There is a Hindu prayer that asks God to "lead us from the unreal to the real, lead us from darkness into light, from death to immortality". Discuss the meaning of these words in class. Design an invitation to an arti service at the mandir. Use the words of the prayer, symbols, pictures and text to explain the service and to encourage people to come.*

3 *Write a poem about the gift of light and what it means to you.*

ELEVEN

Offering food

In this unit you will think about the way in which people have special rules and rituals concerning eating and food. You will also learn about how the beliefs of Hindus influence their diet and their customs regarding food and eating.

People have all sorts of beliefs and customs regarding food. There are theories about what is good for you. There are rules about when to eat and how to eat. People have rituals for preparing and eating food. People have different diets and different tastes.

1 *Write down ten examples of rules, customs and rituals regarding food and drink. These may be your own or those of people you know. Discuss which are religious, which are cultural or social and which are personal. Design a symbol to indicate each of these and mark each rule or ritual with a symbol.*

Families usually follow a diet that is influenced by the traditions of the parents or grandparents. Most Hindu families have their roots in India and so the food they eat reflects their background. In a Hindu home there are certain religious rituals regarding food. Cleanliness is important.

Those involved in preparing food must wash carefully before they cook. In parts of India where the caste system is still in place Hindus will not eat food prepared by anyone from a lower caste or social group. This custom goes back to ancient religious laws regarding purity.

Hindus offer the food they are going to eat to God. Once the meal has been prepared a small portion of each dish is presented at the family shrine. This is an act of love and devotion and a way of giving thanks to God for all his gifts.

> ❝ A little of each dish is placed before the deity. We say prayers and give thanks to God. The food becomes blessed and is returned to the table. It is mixed in with the meal again and the whole meal is blessed by God. ❞
> *[Bharti, 12]*

A shrine in a Hindu home in the UK.

Most Hindus are vegetarian and eat no meat at all. One of the reasons for this is that they believe that animals, like human beings, have souls. Vegetarianism also demonstrates compassion and respect for all creatures.

> " Animals have souls. They are on the same path as us but not as far along the road. It is possible for a person to come back in another life as an animal. This is one reason why we do not eat meat. "
> [Sushila, 14]

2 *List all the foods we can get from the cow which do not involve killing the animal. Discuss your findings in class.*

The cow is sacred in India. Hindus very rarely eat beef. The cow is a symbol of goodness and fruitfulness. She provides people with food and drink and her dung is used as fuel, as a fertiliser and a building material. Bulls and cows are important in terms of pulling carts and other farming equipment. Not eating beef is a way of showing respect and gratitude for all the animal gives to human life.

> " When I went to India I was amazed to see cows drinking at the water fountains. Gandhi said that the cow is India's gift to the world. The people of India remember and respect Gandhi as a man of peace who gave them their independence. "
> [Kamal, 15]

3 *What did Mahatma Gandhi mean about the cow being India's gift to the world? If you wanted to give people a symbol or reminder of the importance of respecting the natural world what would you choose? Write your answer in the form of a letter to a newspaper. Or, if you prefer, design a car sticker to give the same message, and write a paragraph to explain your logo.*

What does the cow give to the people of India?

TWELVE

Showing reverence and respect

In this unit you will consider what it is that commands your respect. You will also learn how Hindus show respect and reverence to others.

When Hindus greet one another they bow in respect and with hands together say "Namaste". This means, "I show reverence to you". Hindus believe that God is present in every living being. It is therefore appropriate to show respect and reverence.

Hindus in the UK greeting each other. How can you tell this is a way of expressing reverence and respect?

 To whom do you show respect? Why do you respect them? How do you show your respect? Write your answers to these questions in full sentences and then compare notes with a partner.

In Hinduism showing respect and reverence for others is considered important. Children are taught to show reverence and respect towards parents and elders. Showing reverence means acknowledging greatness or holiness in someone. When Hindus show reverence to a person they may bow down or touch that person's feet when they greet them.

" When my grandparents come to visit from India we rush to touch their feet before they hug us. We believe we owe a lot to our parents and grandparents. They are wiser than us and they deserve our love and respect. [*Champa, 13*]

At the temple we show reverence when we approach the priest. He is a wise, holy and highly educated man but he has remained a truly humble person. We bow and touch the ground beneath his feet as a sign of respect. " [*Tara, 17*]

2 ▶ *Showing reverence or respect towards people is unusual nowadays. However, there are still some people who command our respect. What is it that makes a person great or holy – how is it different from just being famous like a film or pop star? Write a conversation between two people about this question. Include a discussion on which people have been recognised as truly great or holy.*

A Hindu child shows respect to someone older.

" According to our tradition, we must always show respect to our parents and elders. Secondly we should show respect to visitors who have come a long way, especially uninvited guests, and thirdly to animals and all living creatures.
[*Bhavna, 15*]

When we went to visit India we were treated like royalty. Total strangers showed us places to visit, they took us into their homes, fed us and showered us with gifts. "
[*Meena, 14*]

Throughout the history of Hinduism there have been great religious teachers. These holy men and women are known as gurus. When a guru or holy person comes to preach or to visit the local community he or she is welcomed with garlands of fresh flowers. Showing respect to important people in this way is a traditional practice throughout India.

3 ▶ *"Showing respect to others encourages others to show respect to you." Do you think this is true? Write a set of guidelines for your school on how people can show respect to one another. Give reasons for developing this practice of showing respect.*

Giving flower garlands is a way of showing respect.

THIRTEEN

Following a leader

In this unit you will reflect on the people and teachers that influence the way you live your life. You will also learn about the importance of a teacher or guru for many Hindus.

1 *Which people most influence you and the way you see the world? Is it parents or guardians, teachers or famous personalities such as pop stars or footballers? How do they influence you and the way you think and behave? Write your answers. Read your answer to a partner.*

In Hinduism there is a tradition of seeking guidance from gurus. The word "guru" means "from darkness to light". Gurus are men and women who may have spent many years practising meditation, reading the scriptures and searching for the truth about life. Through listening to their teachings and drawing on their personal experience others can learn from them and develop their own religious or spiritual lives.

Sathya Sai Baba with his followers at his ashram.

66 I follow the teachings of Sri Sathya Sai Baba. He has helped me to understand my religion better. He has also helped me to see truth in the religious paths of others. Sai Baba has performed many miracles and has influenced the lives of Hindus throughout the world. [*Ashok, 18*]

The Hindu religion can work at different levels. You can carry out the daily acts of worship at the shrine and express your religion in this way. Or you can go deeper and develop skills in meditation and yoga and learn about the teachings of the scriptures. For this you need a guru. 99
[*Rupa, 19*]

2 *Some people talk about the spiritual path in life. What do you think they mean by this? Which of the following activities might help people on their spiritual path:*

- *Shopping?*
- *Helping others?*
- *Spending time in quiet reflection?*
- *Making money?*
- *Spending money?*
- *Reading the scriptures?*
- *Watching violent movies on TV?*
- *Listening to the words of religious teachers?*

Discuss your answers in class.

In India there are religious centres called ashrams. These are residential centres set up around a communal way of life. Often these ashrams are based on the teaching and example of a guru. Some gurus have an international reputation. Their teachings are widely known and they travel to visit Hindu communities all over the world. Gopal, who is 21, said: "We went to India and stayed in an ashram. There was a simple routine that allowed you to organise your day around prayer and meditation. In the evening we attended lectures given by the guru."

3 Design a poster to advertise the arrival of a guru at the local Hindu temple. Say which aspects of Hinduism are going to be addressed – for example "Meditation" or "Brahman and Atman". Look back through the book for a suitable topic.

4 For some people Gandhi was the greatest religious leader of this century. Find out about his life and his teachings and the ashram he set up. Write a mini-project on him.

Hindu holy men at an ashram in India.

FOURTEEN

Looking at creation

1 ▶ *Do you ever think about how the world began? What is your view about how things came into being? Do you know any theories or stories about creation? What are they? Write your answers to these questions and discuss your responses in class.*

Hindus believe that the universe goes through cycles. There are four different ages which they call "yugas". These last for millions of years. Within these cycles there are times which might be called golden when truth and goodness reign. At other times goodness struggles against evil and there are times of darkness like the present. A dark age is called a "Kali yuga". At the end of each cycle of time the universe is dissolved. Then follows the long sleep of Vishnu before everything is re-created and the cycle begins again.

Looking at the stars may make us ask questions about how things began.

> There are several creation stories in Hinduism. The one I like best begins with Vishnu sleeping on a great serpent. It makes me think about what it was like at the beginning.
>
> [Dinesh, 11]

In the beginning there was only a vast and empty ocean. Lord Vishnu lay resting in the coils of a great serpent which was floating on the waters. A sound stirred him from his sleep: Aummmmm. Out of Vishnu's navel grew a lotus flower and from its centre appeared the four-headed Brahma. His task was to serve Lord Vishnu by creating the universe. Vishnu departed and left Brahma to start work. Brahma divided the lotus into three and from them he created the heavens, the earth and the skies. He filled the earth with all kinds of plants. Then he made all the creatures of the world including humankind.

Brahma emerges from the lotus flower growing out of Vishnu's navel.

 Tell this story of creation in your own words using the text and the illustration to help you. If you prefer, you can tell it in words and pictures as a story book for Hindu children.

The Hindu view of creation does not put humans at the centre of the universe. Nor do Hindus see humans as the highest form of life. They believe that all creatures have a right to life and they must care for and show respect for the life around them, since Brahman is present in all living beings. Twelve-year-old Anand said: "If we destroy the environment and show no respect to the world around us we are showing disrespect to God."

 Make a leaflet to advertise a talk at the Hindu temple to raise awareness about environmental issues. Make sure you include references to Hindu beliefs about God, creation and living creatures.

FIFTEEN

Going round in circles

In this unit you will think about how life goes in cycles. You will also consider the Hindu belief in samsara, the cycle of rebirth.

In this funeral procession the body is being carried to the cremation pyre. At cremation the body returns to the elements but the soul moves on.

> **1** ▸ *The cycle of night and day, the cycle of one generation following another – what other cycles in life are there? Write down your examples. Compare your answers with those of a partner or friend.*

Hindus believe that everyone has a soul that survives the death of the body and returns to live again in a new body. Every living creature is born, lives, dies and is reborn. So all life is caught in a cycle. This cycle of life, death and rebirth is called "samsara".

A perpetual cycle of life might sound like a good idea at first. However, Hindus see this cycle of birth, death and rebirth as a chain of suffering.

> **2** ▸ *Is it possible to live without suffering? How would living over and over again increase suffering? If you knew you were going to be reborn how would you feel about it? Discuss these questions with a partner and then write your answers to the questions.*

> ❝ Birth brings suffering with it. You cannot escape suffering. The only answer is to break free from the chains of samsara. ❞
> [Ela, 15]

3 Draw a circle of links in a chain to represent the idea of a cycle of rebirth. Around the circle write birth, life, death, rebirth. Write a paragraph underneath to explain the Hindu belief in samsara. Say why Hindus want to break free from these chains.

Hindus believe that they are caught up in this chain of events because every action they make helps to turn the wheels of samsara. It is very hard to break the cycle of samsara because it is impossible to stop acting. The ultimate aim of every Hindu is "moksha". Moksha is liberation. To attain moksha is to break free from the chains of samsara.

" Moksha is freedom. It is when the soul is released from the chains of rebirth and free to be united with Brahman – free to be one with God. "
[Mukta, 19]

4 Represent moksha in a picture or diagram – you could adapt your diagram of the chains of samsara or you could design a new one to represent the idea of breaking free.

above: Hindus believe that everyone has lived before – even the smallest child is not at the beginning of the life cycle.

right: The cycle of life is clear in the seasons of nature. Hindus see human life as a cycle too.

SIXTEEN

Acting and becoming

In this unit you will consider whether everything we do has an effect on us. You will find out about the Hindu belief in the law of karma.

 1 *If a person smokes 100 cigarettes a day, they shorten their life. If someone tells lies, they lose the trust of their friends. If a person eats only sweets, they destroy their teeth. Write six more examples or draw cartoons to illustrate how it could be said that we are to some extent a result of what we have made ourselves by our own actions.*

According to Hinduism everything we do has an effect on us. This is called karma. Karma means action or the result of actions. Hindus believe that karma is stored in such a way that it follows a being from one life to the next. A person does not know when good or bad karma from a previous existence will surface in life.

A diagram to show the connection between actions and their effects on future experiences.

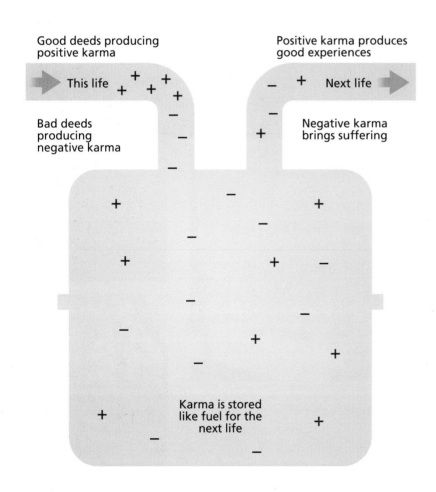

Good deeds producing positive karma

Positive karma produces good experiences

This life

Next life

Bad deeds producing negative karma

Negative karma brings suffering

Karma is stored like fuel for the next life

66 If my actions are good, I build up good or positive karma. If I do mean or selfish things, I build up bad or negative karma. My karma will determine what happens to me in the future.
[Mukesh, 14]

The kind of person we are in the next life depends on how we have acted in this and in previous lives.
[Poonam, 13]

Sometimes our bad karma doesn't catch up with us straight away. We may not pay for our bad deeds until a future life. 99
[Asha, 16]

The belief in karma is basic to Hinduism. It helps to explain why some people are born into a life of suffering and others into a life of comfort. Everyone has the life they have made for themselves.

This man's experience in this life is one of poverty and suffering. What explanation might a Hindu give for his suffering?

 2 *Draw a diagram to represent the process of karma. You could use the one here to help you or you could design your own way of representing the process. Write a few sentences to explain your diagram.*

3
- *"He had it coming to him."*
- *"His deeds have come back to haunt him."*
- *"You've made your bed, now lie in it."*

Do we all believe in a kind of law of karma? Write a short role-play in which a Hindu explains the meaning of the law of karma to a friend who is not a Hindu. Use the text and the quotations to help you with the conversation.

SEVENTEEN

Doing what is right

In this unit you will reflect on the different duties people have. You will learn about the Hindu idea of dharma and consider whether it is similar to the idea of duty.

One of the most important concepts in Hinduism is dharma. The word dharma means law, or religion, or what is right. Hindus believe that everything in creation follows certain laws or principles. Everything has a dharma. It is the dharma of fire to burn. It is the dharma of the sheepdog to round up animals.

Hindus believe that every human being has a dharma or duty. The dharma of each individual depends on who they are, their ability, and their stage in life.

 Most people have a sense of duty or responsibility. A parent feels a duty to care and provide for his/her children. A doctor has a sense of duty when someone needs medical help. Write six examples of your own. Discuss your ideas in class.

There are many Hindu stories which demonstrate the importance of following one's duty or dharma. The most well known is that of Prince Rama. Thirteen-year-old Lakshman said, "Rama is an example for us. We must, like him, try our best to fulfil our dharma in life."

❝ I am a school student so my dharma is to study hard and do well in my school work. My dharma will be different when I am married.
[*Krishna, 14*]

As a priest it is my duty to carry out the rituals at the temple and to help the people in religious and spiritual matters. ❞
[*Rajan Parekh, 44*]

The dharma or duty of the priest is to serve the spiritual needs of the people – what might this involve?

There was once a king. When he was growing old he arranged for his son Rama to inherit the throne. However, Rama's stepmother was determined that her son should follow in the king's place. The king owed her two favours so she went to him and made him promise to send Rama into exile for fourteen years and to make her son king. The king kept his promises and died broken-hearted. The people wanted Rama as king but his duty as a son was to keep his father's word. He went into exile in the forest with his devoted wife Sita and his brother. Although the sensible thing seemed to be to overrule the queen, the right thing was to be obedient to his father. The queen's son ruled in Rama's place but put Rama's slippers on the throne. He knew it was not his dharma to become king.

While Rama was in exile the demon Ravana kidnapped Sita and took her away to his palace in Lanka. With the help of his brother and an army of monkeys Rama rescued Sita and destroyed Ravana and his evil demons. After fourteen years in the forest Rama was able to return to his kingdom. Rama's reign was a golden age of peace, abundance and righteousness.

Rama and Sita returned to reign in peace.

2 *Our duties often correspond to our relationships. Draw yourself on a page and indicate the people around you with whom you are in contact. Write in the duties and responsibilities you have towards each of these people.*

3 *Write your own story on dharma where someone fulfils their duty or responsibilities rather than doing what suits them. Role play or act out your stories in class.*

EIGHTEEN

Belonging

In this unit you will think about the ways in which people belong to different groups. You will learn about the ancient Hindu caste system which divides people into groups.

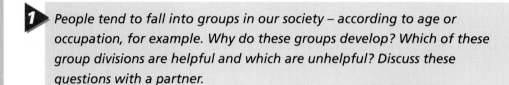

1 *People tend to fall into groups in our society – according to age or occupation, for example. Why do these groups develop? Which of these group divisions are helpful and which are unhelpful? Discuss these questions with a partner.*

In the Hindu scriptures there is a story about the sacrifice of a giant called "Primal Man". From his body four groups were created. The priests, called brahmins, were made from his mouth. The royalty and military, called kshatriyas, came from his arms. The merchant and business class, called the vaishyas, were made from his thighs. The servant class, called shudras, came from his feet. These four groups were called the four "varnas".

This model helped to explain the importance of different roles and responsibilities in society. The brahmins had to take care of the religious and spiritual needs of the community. The kshatriyas were responsible for the peace and security of the land. The duty of the vaishyas was to ensure prosperity, trade and development. The shudras were responsible for providing the many different services needed in society. When everyone fulfilled their duty then society would run smoothly.

These four classes or varnas provided the pattern for society in early India. The four varnas became subdivided into many smaller groups or castes called jatis. These represented the many different occupations.

Brahmins (priests)

Kshatriyas (princes and warriors)

Vaishyas (business people and merchants)

Shudras (servants)

Why do you think the story says the servants came from the feet of the giant and the warriors from the arms?

Gandhi with crowds gathered around him. Find out more about what he tried to do for oppressed people.

> " Every society has its leaders, its business class, people who serve and people who are served. India is no different in this respect. [*Champa, 18*]

> In India, especially in the villages, the caste system is still in place but here in the UK we do not pay much attention to caste divisions. It is racism that creates division here. " [*Jyoti, 15*]

 Society would not function if, for example, everyone was a leader or a shopkeeper or a social worker. Write a story for children to explain how different people have different roles and different jobs to do and everyone's contribution is needed.

According to Hindu tradition a person was born into a caste and stayed in the caste of their family for life. In India some groups of people became known as outcastes. It was believed that their occupations made them unfit for mixing in society. For many years they faced discrimination and were unable to move up in society. In India today, discrimination against outcastes is illegal. Gandhi called outcastes Harijans, or Children of God. He tried to change the system to improve their position in society. The name they have chosen for themselves is "Dallit", which means "oppressed".

 In which ways are all people equal? In which ways are they different? Discuss these questions in class. Write your answers to each question after the discussion.

NINETEEN

Growing up

 1 *How do you see life dividing up into times and seasons? Draw a circle and divide it up like a cake with each section representing a different period of life and write in the various stages of life as you see them. Illustrate your diagram if you wish with symbols to represent the times of life.*

The Hindu scriptures refer to the four stages of life. The first is the student stage. The second is a time for earning a living, marriage and raising a family. The third stage is retirement and the last is a time to prepare for death.

 2 *What special occasions are celebrated in the life of a young person? Write your answer in full sentences. Share your ideas in class and add to your answer.*

The student stage is a time of learning. According to Hindu tradition, when the young person is old enough to take responsibility for their own behaviour, it is time for them to learn about the beliefs and practices of their religion. In some Hindu families there is a special ceremony to mark this time. It is the Upanayana or the Sacred Thread Ceremony.

In the past the Upanayana marked the time when the Hindu boy left home to go and study under a guru. (Nowadays the young person does not have to leave home.) The priest leads the ceremony. A fire is lit and offerings are made to God. The boy wears white, a symbol of purity. Usually he fasts before the ceremony. Prayers are said and the boy learns to recite the Gayatri Mantra. "May the eternal light of the universe enlighten our minds and hearts."

3 *The symbol of light is often used to represent learning. Design a symbol for young people to show that they are in the student stage of life – people who are learning.*

The father places a thread knotted with three strands across the left shoulder of his son. This hangs diagonally across the chest. The sacred thread is worn by vaishyas, kshatriyas and brahmins. The young person makes a vow of celibacy (to refrain from sexual activity). He promises to take seriously his dharma as a student. This will mean spending time reading the scriptures and learning the practices of prayer and meditation.

" It was quite an important ceremony for me. I had to learn more about my religion and it made me think about my beliefs.
[*Mukesh, 12*]

After the ceremony we had a celebration with family and friends. I had been fasting so I was hungry. "
[*Rajan, 12*]

4 *Imagine you are a reporter gathering news for a small local paper. You are at the party following the Sacred Thread Ceremony. Interview different people who were present at the occasion to find out more about the ceremony and its meaning. Write your account as a series of mini interviews. Use the photograph and the text to help you.*

A Hindu boy learns about the sacred thread that he will wear.

Taking responsibility for others

1 *What are the responsibilities that you have taken on in the last five years that you did not have before? What new responsibilities will you take on in the next five years? What are the good things about responsibilities? What are the bad things about them? Answer the questions in sentences. Read your sentences to a partner.*

In the life of a Hindu, there are religious guidelines about the appropriate responsibilities for each stage in life. These are written in the scriptures called the Laws of Manu. According to these texts the responsibilities of one stage must be fulfilled before commencing with the next. Following the student stage comes that of the householder.

> 66 I have finished my degree and now I'm training to be a lawyer. I'm engaged but I must complete my studies before I take on the responsibilities of marriage and family life. 99
> [*Kirpan, 23*]

Running a home includes taking responsibility for the religious life of the family.

Marriage brings new responsibilities. Earning a living, running a home, raising children: these are important according to Hindu tradition. So too are daily religious duties and contributing to the life of the community.

> 66 My mother prays at the shrine in the front room in the morning then she wakes us and gets breakfast. Later she helps with the toddler group at the mandir. My father works at the hospital. He often stops at the mandir on his way home. 99
> [*Meena, 12*]

A Hindu household is often made up of three generations. Hindus believe that it is the responsibility of children to look after their parents when they are in their old age.

The grandparents remain within the family in a Hindu home – what does that tell you about the duties and responsibilities of the householder?

" My grandparents live with us. My grandmother helps in the house. She does not work in the shop any more. My grandfather has a bad hip and can't get about. My parents have to look after him and run the shop so they're very busy. "
[Vaneela, 13]

2 Put the hours of the day down the left-hand margin of a page – beginning at 6 am. Fill in a day in the life of a Hindu couple who are taking seriously the responsibilities of the householder stage in life. Look back at previous units to help you to draw up a day in the life of a Hindu household.

3 Do you think that young people think carefully about the responsibilities involved before they get married? Design a poster aimed at young people to help prepare them for the responsibilities of the householder stage in life.

TWENTY-ONE

Getting married

In this unit you will consider the importance of thinking carefully about marriage. You will learn about the Hindu wedding ceremony and the meaning of the customs and rituals.

 Will you marry? If you do how will you choose your marriage partner? What will you look for and how will you make sure that you find the right person? Write your answer in full sentences. Read your notes to a friend or partner.

It is usual for Hindu parents to be involved in helping their son or daughter find a marriage partner. They will look for someone from the same kind of family background. To avoid the risk of an unhappy marriage the parents take the views of the young people into account before a final decision is made.

❝ My parents introduced me to someone a year ago. He was a nice person but I knew I could not be happy with him. So they looked again and arranged for me to meet the son of some friends of theirs. His name is Rama. We like each other a lot and we are going to be married next year. ❞
[Dipa, 21]

Hindu wedding ceremonies vary from one community to another as many of the traditional customs are social or cultural in origin. Some rituals and symbols carry religious significance and have their origins in the scriptures.

❝ There is always a fire at the centre of the Hindu wedding ceremony. It represents the power and presence of God. The flames are also a symbol of purity and love. ❞
[Manjula, 18]

The photos in this unit show two different stages in the Hindu marriage ceremony. Identify the stages and describe what is happening.

The wedding ceremony is usually held at the bride's home in India. In the United Kingdom the local mandir or Hindu community centre may be hired for the event. The bride usually wears a red and gold sari. Red is a symbol of life. Her sisters, cousins and female friends help her to get ready. Before the ceremony begins she must be asked whether she accepts the groom as her husband.

The priest leads the ceremony with prayers from the scriptures. He lights a fire, and offerings of water, ghee and rice are sprinkled on the flames. The couple sit next to each other and they are joined by a silk scarf or, alternatively, their clothes are knotted together as a symbol of their union.

The bride and groom take seven steps together. With each step they make a prayer or promise. These express their hopes for happiness, children, prosperity, nutritious food, strength, long life and love.

> " The ceremony is a very special occasion – I was very nervous. Everyone's eyes are on you. You are making a commitment for life but everyone is there to show they support you.
> [Asha, 21]
>
> Marriage should be for life. It is a union of body, mind and heart. It is important to respect one another and to try to meet the needs of your partner. "
> [Manu, 25]

After the wedding ceremony there is a meal for friends and family. In India the celebrations may go on for several days.

2 *Design an invitation to a Hindu wedding. Use Hindu symbols, including the symbols from the ceremony – fire, the colour red, the knotted scarf, the seven steps – to illustrate your work.*

3 *Write a dialogue between a Hindu couple and another couple in which they compare wedding ceremonies – you could imagine that they are looking at wedding photos as a conversation starter.*

elebrating

In this unit you will reflect on the way in which celebrations and festivals are important for many people. You will also learn about a famous festival that is important to Hindus.

1 ▸ *Imagine the government put a ban on all celebrations and festivals. Anyone caught celebrating would be imprisoned. Write out ten points of protest for a flyer asking for the decision to be reversed – state your reasons clearly.*

One of the best loved of Hindu festivals is Janmashtami. It is the birthday of Lord Krishna. Hindus believe that Vishnu came to earth in the form of Krishna. Festivals are times for feasting and celebration. They are also times when Hindus reflect on the stories and teachings of their faith.

Long ago in the city of Mathura on the River Jumna there lived a cruel and evil king called Kamsa. He had been warned that he would be slain by a son born of his cousin Devaki. So Kamsa had his cousin thrown into prison and killed all her children. While Devaki was in prison she gave birth to a boy whose skin was as dark as the night and she called him Krishna, meaning "the dark one". His father, Vasudeva, hid him in a basket and escaped into the night while the guards were asleep. Outside a storm was raging and Vasudeva had to get across the river. The waters raged violently. Then the baby Krishna put his toe into the water. Immediately the waves calmed down and Vasudeva was able to cross safely. He swapped Krishna for the baby girl of a cowherd, Nanda, while he and his wife Yashoda were asleep. Kamsa discovered the trick and gave orders for all new born boys to be slain. But Nanda and Yashoda had moved away from Mathura to Gokula and Krishna grew up safely. Eventually he would return to destroy Kamsa and to establish righteousness and peace.

The birth of Krishna is celebrated in most UK temples with the arti ceremony.

Krishna's father carries him to safety. Tell the story in words and pictures.

66 At Janmashtami we worship the child Krishna. Images of Krishna as a baby remind us that God came to earth as a human being and lived among ordinary people. 99
[*Renu, 17*]

2 ▶ *A baby is a powerful image. Many adverts use a young child or a baby to sell products. Why? What is special about a baby? Is a baby like a god in some ways? Why is a baby a good symbol for God? Discuss answers to these questions in class.*

At Janmashtami images of Krishna are dressed in fine clothes and garlands. Offerings of money, flowers and food are presented. Prayers are said and worshippers gather to sing bhajans and to join in a service of arti.

66 Krishna was born in the middle of the night so the mandir stays open right through the night at Janmashtami. We get to stay up late and we sing hymns called bhajans.
[*Mukta, 14*]

The birthday of Lord Krishna is a big event at our temple. We have an arti service at night. The next day we have a big feast to celebrate. It is a very special time for us. 99
[*Ela, 16*]

3 ▶ *Imagine you have been to the mandir with a Hindu friend for the festival of Janmashtami. Describe what happens at the festival and explain the story and its meaning.*

4 ▶ *Write a mini project on another Hindu festival of your choice.*

TWENTY-THREE

Receiving and remembering

In this unit you will think about the way in which you are able to remember stories. You will also learn about the Hindu scriptures and how they are remembered and taught to others.

1 Can you tell any stories from memory? Which ones? Why do you think you can remember these? Discuss your answers in class.

The most sacred Hindu scriptures are the Vedas. These date back to before 2000 BCE. The Vedas contain hymns and ritual prayers to various deities and they are used in Hindu worship today.

The chapters at the end of the Vedas are called the "Upanishads". Upanishad means "sit down near". Long ago disciples sat down near their guru or teacher and listened to teachings about the nature of Brahman and the meaning of life. These teachings are contained in the Upanishads.

The Vedas and Upanishads belong to the group of scriptures called "shruti", meaning "revealed". It is believed that these teachings were revealed to the holy men of the past.

A Brahmin (priest) reading from the Hindu scriptures

" Some of our scriptures are very, very ancient. They were passed on by word of mouth long before they were written down. In fact the Vedas are the oldest known scriptures in daily use.
[Bharat, 17]

The Vedas are written in Sanskrit. This is the ancient language of India. The priests know and understand the full meaning of the words. We know some of the hymns by heart and of course we can read the translation. "
[Jayesh, 16]

There is another group of scriptures which are called "smriti" or "remembered". These come in the form of stories and guidance for living. The most famous is the Mahabharata, which is a story about the five brave and righteous Pandava brothers who are tricked out of their homeland by their evil and selfish cousins the Kauravas. In the end good wins over evil. (Look at the pages opposite, and pages 50–51.)

The other famous story of the smriti scriptures is the Ramayana, which is the story of Prince Rama. Both the Mahabharata and the Ramayana teach about the importance of dharma. Many of the characters are role models and Hindus try to learn from and follow their example. The Laws of Manu are also included among the sacred texts. These offer guidance on all aspects of life.

    "" The stories from the Mahabharata are acted out in dance and drama in India, so that people can understand the meaning and learn from the teachings of the scriptures.
[*Anita, 16*]

I have a set of comic strip books which tell the stories of the scriptures in cartoon strips. They are really good – they help me to understand the teachings of my religion. **""**
[*Dipa, 12*]

2▶ *Put two headings: Shruti and Smriti. List the different scriptures under each heading and write brief notes on each to show the main differences between the two types of scripture in Hinduism.*

3▶ *Look at the pictures and the quotations in this unit. Write a set of questions you could ask a Hindu about their scriptures. Exchange your questions with those of a partner and write the answers.*

Some Hindus read the stories from the sacred texts in comic book form. In this illustration and in those on pages 50–51 we see scenes from the story in the Mahabharata where Lord Krishna appears to Arjuna who is leading the Pandavas to battle against the Kauravas.

TWENTY-FOUR

War and peace

 When is it right to go to war? Write down three conditions for when war might be necessary. When is war not right or just? Write your answer in sentences and then discuss them in class.

The Bhagavad Gita is the most popular of the Hindu scriptures. It is a section of the Mahabharata (look back at page 49) and contains the teachings of Lord Krishna. Bhagavad Gita means "The Song of the Lord".

At this point in the story of the Mahabharata the battle lines are drawn up for the impending war between the Pandava brothers and their wicked cousins the Kauravas. The Kauravas had tricked the Pandavas out of their land. Having failed to get a just settlement by peaceful means the Pandavas were forced to confront the evil Kauravas on the battlefield.

Arjuna, who is the leading archer among the Pandavas, looks across at the enemy lines. He is filled with dread and begins to tremble. He turns to his charioteer, Krishna, and says he cannot fight: these are members of his family, some of them his elders, and slaying them will bring bad karma. Women would be left without protection and families would be destroyed.

Krishna tells Arjuna he must fight for three reasons. Firstly, as a member of the kshatriya caste it is his dharma to fight. Secondly, the warrior who dies in battle will live again in a new body so he will not be destroying the souls of those he kills. Lastly, he must fight without seeking personal gain. He must fight, but for righteousness, not out of hatred, greed or bitterness. There will be no karma if he fights without desire for personal gain.

THE KAURAVA ARMY HAD ELEVEN DIVISIONS AND WAS THUS NUMERICALLY FAR SUPERIOR TO THE PANDAVA ARMY. TO WITHSTAND THE ENEMY ONSLAUGHT, THE PANDAVA ARMY HAD BEEN ARRAYED IN NEEDLE-LIKE FORMATION. ARJUNA WAS IN THE CENTRE IN HIS CHARIOT, TO WHICH HAD BEEN YOKED FOUR WHITE HORSES. KRISHNA WAS HIS CHARIOTEER.

The lines are drawn up for battle against the Kauravas.

 Tell the story of the Pandavas and Kauravas in a version for a Hindu community newsletter for children. Make sure you bring out the teachings of Krishna. Illustrate your article.

At the end of the Gita Krishna reveals his true identity as the avatar of Vishnu and as the Supreme Lord. The Pandavas go on to win the battle and peace and justice are established.

In the Bhagavad Gita, going to war is the last resort. All peaceful negotiations have failed. There is no attack on civilians, and only trained warriors fight in the battle. The war is not for power but to provide security for the citizens. Later in Indian history Gandhi encouraged his people to achieve independence for India by peaceful means. He demonstrated the value of "ahimsa" which means "not harming" or "non-violence".

> ❝ We put great emphasis on not harming others – that is, "ahimsa". So we try to avoid violence in all aspects of life. For example, we do not kill for meat.
> [Sita, 14]
>
> Ahimsa means more than not using force. Cruel words can cause harm so we should try not to hurt others in any way. ❞
> [Ashok, 13]

3 ▸ Imagine you want to make "ahimsa" a motto for our society – how would you go about it? Write a protest song or make a T-shirt design to put across the idea of ahimsa.

THE GITA

AS ARJUNA LOOKED UP, THE LIGHT DAZZLED HIM. HE SAW IN IT ALL BEINGS. IT SEEMED TO HIM AS IF HE WERE LOOKING AT CREATION; THE WHOLE OF CREATION; EVERYTHING IN CREATION; LOOKING AT THE WHOLE OF THE PAST; THE WHOLE OF THE PRESENT AND THE WHOLE OF THE FUTURE – ALL AT ONCE. IT WAS A SIGHT NO MAN HAD SEEN BEFORE. IT STAGGERED AND STUPEFIED HIM. HE WAS AS IF THE OBSERVER OF THE WHOLE DRAMA OF LIFE.

Krishna reveals himself as the Supreme Lord.

TWENTY-FIVE

Doing, thinking, feeling

In this unit you will consider different ways in which people find meaning and purpose in their lives. You will hear what Lord Krishna had to say on the three ways to union with God.

 1 *Does life have meaning and purpose? What are the ways in which people find meaning in their lives? Is it through their family; is it through their work? Write six examples of ways in which people look for meaning and purpose in life.*

In the Bhagavad Gita Krishna speaks of three ways to live a life that has meaning and purpose. These are the ways that lead to moksha, to liberation from karma and rebirth. They lead to union with Brahman. In other words they lead to God.

The three ways are called the three "yogas". The first is karma yoga – the way of action. You can carry out your daily work and fulfil your duty in life. But all your actions must be free from selfish desire, free from greed and hatred. If you act for selfish reasons bad karma follows. But free from selfish desire you are free from karma. This is one way to moksha or liberation.

> ❝ Usually our deeds are driven by the desire to help ourselves or, worse still, to hurt others. We must give up these selfish thoughts and intentions if we want to follow the path of unselfish action. ❞
> [Naresh, 18]

The second way is jnana yoga – the way of knowledge. This means giving up the comforts and selfish attachments of life. It requires self-discipline, self-sacrifice, meditation and yoga. In this way a person burns up past karma and reaches moksha.

> ❝ For most of us the way of knowledge is too hard. It requires cutting yourself off from the world, fasting and meditating for long periods – I would find it very difficult. ❞
> [Ravi, 16]

How can a nurse follow the teachings of Krishna in her work?

2 If you are committed to a cause, a person or a religion, it often means giving up something. Can you think of any examples? Write a story or poem on this idea of sacrifice.

The third way that Krishna talked about was bhakti yoga. Bhakti means selfless, loving devotion. Through reciting God's name and singing his praises and dedicating every action to him the worshipper becomes closer and closer to God. Ultimately bhakti yoga leads to union with God and liberation from the chains of karma and samsara.

> For most Hindus bhakti is the way to God. Lord Krishna says he will release us from karma and by his grace we will find union with him and enjoy his love and protection. [*Sumitra, 15*]

> Radha was Krishna's closest friend when he was a cowherd in the forests of Vrindavan. Radha loved Krishna so completely she is an example for us. She reminds us that we should love God selflessly and try to stay close to him. [*Geeta, 13*]

3 Draw Radha and Krishna represented by murtis (images) in a shrine. Underneath write a paragraph on their meaning for Hindus.

4 What is the connection between the three paths to moksha? What do they have in common? Use a diagram/pictures/symbols for a design for a banner to show the three ways to travel on the path to moksha.

Some Hindus try to attain moksha through the discipline of yoga and meditation.

right: Krishna with his beloved Radha. In the way of loving devotion the worshipper must love God as Radha loved her Lord Krishna.

TWENTY-SIX

Going places

In this unit you will reflect on the meaning and purpose of pilgrimage. You will also learn about the importance of pilgrimage in the Hindu tradition.

 Write the word "journey" in the centre of a page. Make a spider diagram writing in all the different reasons people go on journeys and the good things and bad things about journeys.

Some journeys are not just about having a holiday. A journey can be an opportunity to reflect on what is important in life. Perhaps this is why pilgrimage is important in many religions.

> ❝ When you go on a pilgrimage you leave your possessions behind. You realise that you don't need them. You only need a few necessities. It puts things in perspective. ❞
> [Prashant, 20]

2 *Some of the baggage we carry around in life we can see. For example, material possessions can become a burden. Some of the baggage that weighs people down cannot be seen. It is still a burden. Divide a page in two. In words and pictures illustrate the different kinds of baggage that people carry.*

Pilgrims bathing in the Ganges at Varanasi.

Pilgrimage is especially important for Hindus in their third stage of life. When they have retired from work they have time to put the spiritual side of life first. This may include fasting, meditation and reading the scriptures. For many Hindus pilgrimage is important at this time in life.

There are many pilgrimage sites in India. The most famous is Varanasi. Some people call it Benares. Pilgrims come to bathe in the River Ganges (also called Ganga) and to visit the shrines and temples. Hindus believe that the water of the Ganges is so sacred it can wash away the karma of past actions. This is why so many Hindus come to Varanasi as a preparation for death.

> ❝ My grandmother is getting very old and cannot travel, so my father is going to Varanasi to bring back water from the Ganges for her. ❞
> [*Gopal, 16*]

Sometimes a person undertakes a pilgrimage to thank God for an answer to prayer. Others go as an act of love and devotion to a particular god or goddess. An important part of pilgrimage is seeing the deity at the shrine or temple. This is called "darshan". Another aspect of pilgrimage is buying postcards and souvenirs – but this is never the main purpose of the journey.

> ❝ Our friends went to India, to Vrindavan, the homeland of Krishna. They went to give thanks to Lord Krishna for their new baby. ❞
> [*Ela, 21*]

Hindus do not have to travel to India to go on a pilgrimage. There are now places in the United Kingdom where Hindus go and find the same sense of community and shared religious experience.

> ❝ We went on a pilgrimage to Bhaktivedanta Manor near Watford in Hertfordshire for the celebration of Krishna's birthday. There were thousands of people, singing and worshipping together. ❞
> [*Ganesh, 11*]

 Find out more about Hindu pilgrimage. Write a TV/radio programme about Hindu pilgrimage. Include "interviews" with pilgrims as well as information you have researched.

Bhaktivedanta Manor in England has become a place of pilgrimage for many Hindus living in the UK.

TWENTY-SEVEN

Giving up the world

In this unit you will reflect on how a person's view of life may change as they get older. You will learn about what is expected in later life in Hindu tradition.

1 *What do most people look forward to in retirement? What do you think you might like to do when you are in your sixties? Write a poem or short story called "When I am sixty-four".*

After the householder stage in life there are two more stages according to Hindu tradition. There is retirement, which begins when the grandchildren come along and sons and daughters are able to take over the responsibilities of running a home. Retirement is an opportunity to concentrate on spiritual matters.

> " There is more time for prayer, for visiting the mandir, for helping others and for reading the scriptures. In this way we can prepare for death and build up good karma. "
> [*Kavita, 19*]

There is another stage beyond retirement according to the Hindu scriptures – but it is generally regarded as voluntary. This is the stage of the sannyasin. Being a sannyasin means leaving behind the comforts of home and the attachments of family. This stage in life is spent travelling, preaching and begging for food. Through fasting, yoga and meditation the karma of past actions can be reversed. Once all karma has been destroyed there will be no coming back in another life. When the soul leaves the body it will be united with Brahman. The goal of the sannyasin is moksha.

The sannyasin carries a bowl because he must rely on the alms that people give him for food.

> " I was a bank manager. After a few years in retirement I left my wife, my son and my grandchildren. I left them the house and possessions. Now I live on the banks of the Ganges. Every day I bathe in the waters. I go to the mandir, I teach, I travel, I study the scriptures and spend time in meditation. I have no worries, there is nothing for me to worry about. I'm happy. I am ready for death. "
> [*Mukesh Sharma, 65*]

The sannyasin spends his time on the road, travelling from place to place and teaching others.

2 Most people prepare for their old age by trying to ensure they will be well-off and comfortable. How does the way of the sannyasin compare with this approach? Which do you think is the more sensible and realistic approach to the end of life? Write your answer in the form of a play or a conversation between a Hindu and someone with a more Western outlook.

3 Draw a diagram representing the four stages in life in Hinduism. (Look at units 19, 20, 21 and 27 to help you.) Use words and pictures to explain the different stages.

4 Can we prepare ourselves for death? Is this something we should take seriously and plan ahead for? Should preparation for death be on the school curriculum? Write a plan for a six-week course that helps people to think about death in a constructive way. You might have visiting speakers, or go to places that you think would be helpful in this process.

TWENTY-EIGHT

Leaving the body

In this unit you will be thinking about the way in which funeral rites can be important and meaningful. You will be finding out about the Hindu cremation ceremony.

 1 When a person dies there usually follows a very busy time for the family. With a partner discuss ten things that will need to be done when a relative dies. Write your answers in full sentences. Listen to the suggestions of others in the class.

2 People usually want to have a ceremony to mark the death of someone they love. What sort of sentiments do people want to express in such a ceremony? Write a prayer or a poem that expresses some of the thoughts and feelings a person might want to convey at a funeral of someone they loved.

In Hinduism cremation rather than burial is the tradition. It is at cremation that the soul is released from the body. So it is essential that the cremation is carried out correctly. It is not just a time for the family; it is important for the soul of the departed. The eldest son of the deceased is responsible for organising the funeral. If there is no son, another male member of the family takes the responsibility. The body is carefully washed and wrapped in a clean white cloth. In India a cremation pyre is built outside, often on the banks of a river.

> " My father and mother were both cremated on the banks of the Ganges. After the cremation the ashes were scattered over the water. They say that if you are cremated there your soul does not return to be born again but is united with God. "
> [Rajesh Desai, 52]

The priest is invited to lead the prayers at the cremation. Family and friends gather around the pyre, and the eldest son lights the fire. Following instructions from the priest he makes offerings of clarified butter (called ghee) and incense into the flames. Texts from the Hindu scriptures are recited reminding everyone present that while the body returns to the different elements the soul is released.

When the cremation is over there is usually a family gathering. Later when the ashes are cool they are collected up and scattered into the waters of the nearest river. In the United Kingdom the family use the services of the local crematorium and afterwards they are given the ashes to take away.

" When I arranged my aunt's funeral at the crematorium the service was simple and I was glad of the help of the people there. But it was very different from how a cremation would be in India. In India you see the body. I think you come to terms with death more because of this. People here do not want to look at death.
[*Sandeep, 32*]

When we first came to the UK the crematoriums had Christian symbols in place and it was difficult to organise the ceremony in a way that was Hindu. Today we have more say in the way things are done; we can invite our priest and have Hindu symbols and prayers. "
[*Suraj Chatterjee, 66*]

3 Write a diary entry in which a tourist describes their visit to Varanasi and sees a cremation take place on the banks of the sacred river Ganges. Say how the scene helped them understand something about the beliefs and practices of Hinduism.

A cremation on the banks of the sacred river Ganges.

TWENTY-NINE

Freeing the spirit

1 *What are your aims in life? Write down six things that you want to achieve or you think will make you content in life. Compare your ideas with those of others. Try to divide the aims into different types, for example fame, wealth, and so on. Write a report on what you have found out about the aims of your class.*

Hindus believe that there are important goals in this life. For example, gaining wealth and success in the world, setting up a comfortable home and enjoying the pleasures prosperity brings. This goal is called "artha". It is a perfectly respectable goal so long as your gains are made by honest means and you contribute to the overall wealth of the community. However, wealth and success in the world cannot bring long-term happiness nor ultimate escape from suffering.

Another aim in life is "kama", the pleasure of a passionate and loving relationship. Hindus believe that the joys of love are very important. A husband must make his wife happy and she must give him pleasure too. However wonderful such a relationship may be, and however long it lasts, like artha, this goal in life cannot bring lasting pleasure or peace.

❝ Our religion does not frown on the rewards of wealth or physical pleasure, nor the joys of having a home and family. But we are warned that these things can tie us down in the chains of samsara. Ultimately they cannot bring lasting happiness nor release us from suffering. ❞
[*Mukta, 24*]

At the festival of Diwali Hindu businessmen make offerings to the goddess of prosperity and good fortune. They pray for success and ask her blessings on the books ready for a new year of business. In this way the first goal in life is given religious blessing.

A third goal is doing what is right, and fulfilling one's responsibilities at each stage in life. For most people it involves raising a family, caring for loved ones and serving the community. This goal, dharma, is held in high esteem in Hinduism and it is explored in the teachings of the Ramayana and the Mahabharata. Fulfilling one's dharma will help one to good karma. This will ensure a better life in the future. However, being born into another life (and another and another . . .) will inevitably bring pain and suffering.

According to the teachings of Hinduism, the ultimate goal in life is moksha. This is release from the suffering of birth and death. Reunited with Brahman the soul experiences unlimited and unending peace and happiness. Hindus believe they are all on the same path, the path that leads to moksha. Some are further along the path than others but all will get there in the end.

To find a close and loving relationship is an important aim in life for many people.

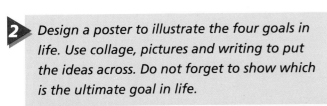

2 *Design a poster to illustrate the four goals in life. Use collage, pictures and writing to put the ideas across. Do not forget to show which is the ultimate goal in life.*

3 *Write a group story about a Hindu who lives through the four stages of life and fulfils the goals of artha, kama, dharma and ultimately moksha.*

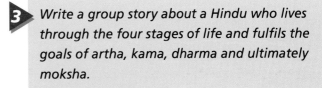

Hindus in joyful celebration at the Ramlila festival. The carriage is conveying Rama to his wedding. Which aims in life does Rama represent?

Glossary

Ahimsa   Belief in non-violence or not-harming

Artha   The second aim in life: gaining success in terms of wealth and worldly achievements

Arti   A welcome ceremony involving offering of light

Ashram   Community based on a religious way of life

Atman   Individual soul or spirit

Aum   Sacred sound and symbol representing the infinite

Avatar   Downcoming or manifestation of God in bodily form

Bhagavad Gita   "The Song of the Lord": a scripture in the Mahabharata

Brahma   The god of creation, one part of the Trimurti

Brahman   The Supreme Spirit, Universal Soul, Ultimate Reality, God

Brahmin   Priest

Darshan   A religious experience involving a sight or vision of the deity

Dharma   Religion, duty, law, what is right

Durga   Hindu goddess representing God as Mother

Gayatri Mantra   A sacred prayer recited in Hindu worship

Guru   Religious teacher, one who leads from darkness to light, who gives enlightenment

Janmashtami   Festival celebrating the birthday of Krishna

Jati   A group in Hindu society traditionally defined by occupation, sometimes called a caste

Kali   Hindu goddess in her most terrifying aspect

Kalki   Avatar of Vishnu yet to come

Kama   The third aim in life: finding pleasure and fulfilment in a passionate and loving relationship

Karma   Action or the result of actions

Krishna   Avatar of Vishnu

Lakshmi   Hindu goddess of prosperity and good fortune

Laws of Manu   Hindu scriptures containing teachings on dharma

Linga   Smooth rounded stone representing Shiva

Mahabharata   Hindu smriti scriptures containing the Bhagavad Gita

Mandir   Hindu temple

Mantra   Prayer or sacred saying

Moksha   Liberation from the cycle of samsara

Murti   Image representing a deity

Puja   Worship often involving offerings at a shrine

Rama   Avatar of Vishnu

Ramayana   The story of Prince Rama from the Hindu smriti scriptures

Samsara   The cycle of birth, life, death and rebirth

Sanatan Dharma   The term Hindus prefer for their religion, meaning eternal law or religion

Sannyasa   The fourth and last stage in life: the life of a wandering ascetic

Shiva   Hindu god, one part of the Trimurti

Shruti   "Revealed": the most sacred of Hindu scriptures

Smriti   "Remembered": Hindu scriptures not contained in Shruti

Trimurti   The three gods Brahma, Vishnu and Shiva

Upanayana   The Sacred Thread Ceremony, a sign of being twice born

Upanishads   Philosophical writings at the end of the Vedas in the Hindu scriptures

Varnas   Classes into which Hindu society was traditionally divided

Vedas   Most ancient and most sacred of Hindu scriptures

Vishnu   Hindu god, one part of the Trimurti

Yantra   Sacred pattern or symbol used in meditation to focus the mind

Yoga   Meaning "discipline": exercise used to discipline mind and body

Yuga   "Age": there are four ages or yugas in the cycle of time

Index

ACKNOWLEDGEMENTS

The author would like to thank Mr Rasmandala Das for helpful suggestions during the preparation of the book for publication.

All the photographs are by courtesy of Bipinchandra Mistry, with the exception of the following:-
pp12, 18 Ann & Bury Peerless, p19 M Briscoe, p27 Adrian Page (bottom), p28 A & B Peerless, p29 Circa/B Mistry, p30 Science Photo Library/ NASA, pp31, 32 A & B Peerless, p33 J Allan Cash (right all), p37 A & B Peerless, p39 Hulton Getty (top), pp44, 45 Adrian Page, p46 D Richardson, p47 A & B Peerless, pp49, 50, 51 Chapel Studios, p52 J Allan Cash, pp56, 60, 61 (bottom) A & B Peerless.

Cover photograph by courtesy of Bipinchandra Mistry

Every reasonable effort has been made to contact copyright owners, but we apologise for any unknown errors or omissions. The list will be corrected, if necessary, in the next printing.

Illustrations and diagrams by Oxford Illustrators.

Oxford University Press, Great Clarendon Street, Oxford OX2 6DP

Oxford New York
Athens Auckland Bangkok Bogota Buenos Aires Calcutta
Cape Town Chennai Dar es Salaam Delhi Florence Hong Kong
Istanbul Karachi Kuala Lumpur Madrid Melbourne Mexico City
Mumbai Nairobi Paris São Paulo Singapore Taipei Tokyo Toronto Warsaw

and associated companies in
Berlin Ibadan

Oxford is a trade mark of Oxford University Press
© Oxford University Press
First published 1998

ISBN 0 19 917254 4

A CIP catalogue record for this book is available from the British Library.

Printed and bound in Hong Kong